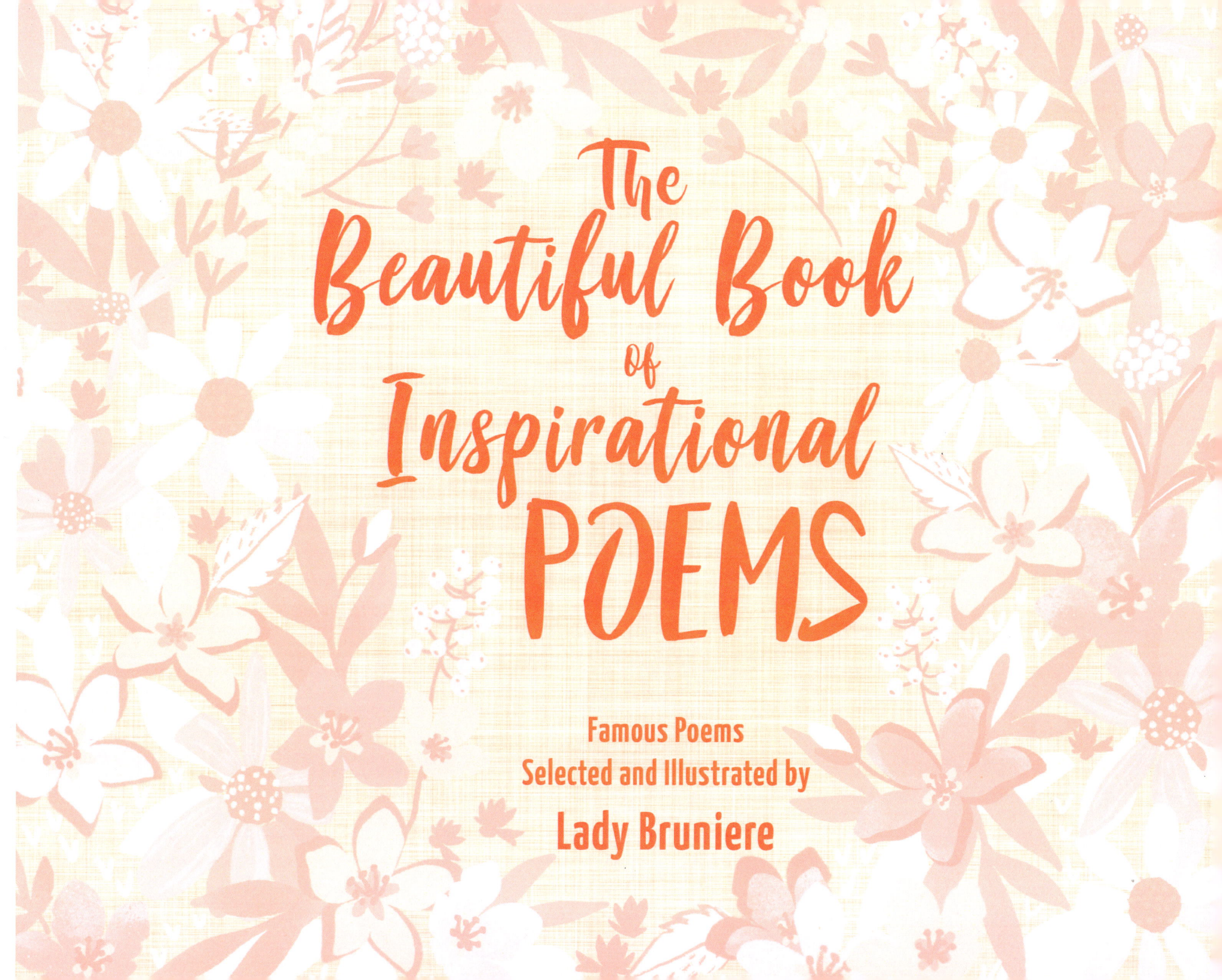

The Beautiful Book of Inspirational POEMS

Famous Poems
Selected and Illustrated by

Lady Bruniere

LADY BRUNIERE

The Wing's Shadow

You who think I don't believe
when we two feud
do not imagine my desire,
my thirst, my hunger for God;

nor have you heard my desolate
cry that echoes through
the inner place of shadow,
calling on the infinite;

nor do you see my thought
laboring in ideal genesis,
frequently in distress
with throes of light.

If my sterile spirit
could own your power of birth,
by now, I would have columned heaven
to perfect your earth.

But tell me, what power stows
within a flagless soul
to carry anywhere at all
its torturer, who knows?

that keeps a fast from faith,
and with valiant integrity
goes on asking every depth
and every darkness, why?

Not with standing, I am shielded
by my thirst for inquiry
my pangs for God, cavernous and unheard;
and there is more love in my unsated
doubt than in your tepid certainty.

Amado Nervo

A Dream

In visions of the dark night
I have dreamed of joy departed
But a waking dream of life and light
Hath left me broken-hearted.

Ah! what is not a dream by day
To him whose eyes are cast
On things around him with a ray
Turned back upon the past?

That holy dream that holy dream,
While all the world were chiding,
Hath cheered me as a lovely beam,
A lonely spirit guiding.

What though that light, thro' storm and night,
So trembled from afar
What could there be more purely bright
In Truth's day star?

Edgar Allan Poe

Hope

Our lives, discoloured with our present woes,
May still grow white and shine with happier hours.
So the pure limped stream, when foul with stains
Of rushing torrents and descending rains,
Works itself clear, and as it runs refines,
till by degrees the floating mirror shines;
Reflects each flower that on the border grows,
And a new heaven in it's fair bosom shows.

Joseph Addison

Shall I compare thee to a summer's day?

Shall I compare thee to a summer's day?
Thou art more lovely and more temperate:
Rough winds do shake the darling buds of May,
And summer's lease hath all too short a date;
Sometime too hot the eye of heaven shines,
And often is his gold complexion dimm'd;
And every fair from fair sometime declines,
By chance or nature's changing course untrimm'd;
But thy eternal summer shall not fade,
Nor lose possession of that fair thou ow'st;
Nor shall death brag thou wander'st in his shade,
When in eternal lines to time thou grow'st:
So long as men can breathe or eyes can see,
So long lives this, and this gives life to thee.

William Shakespeare

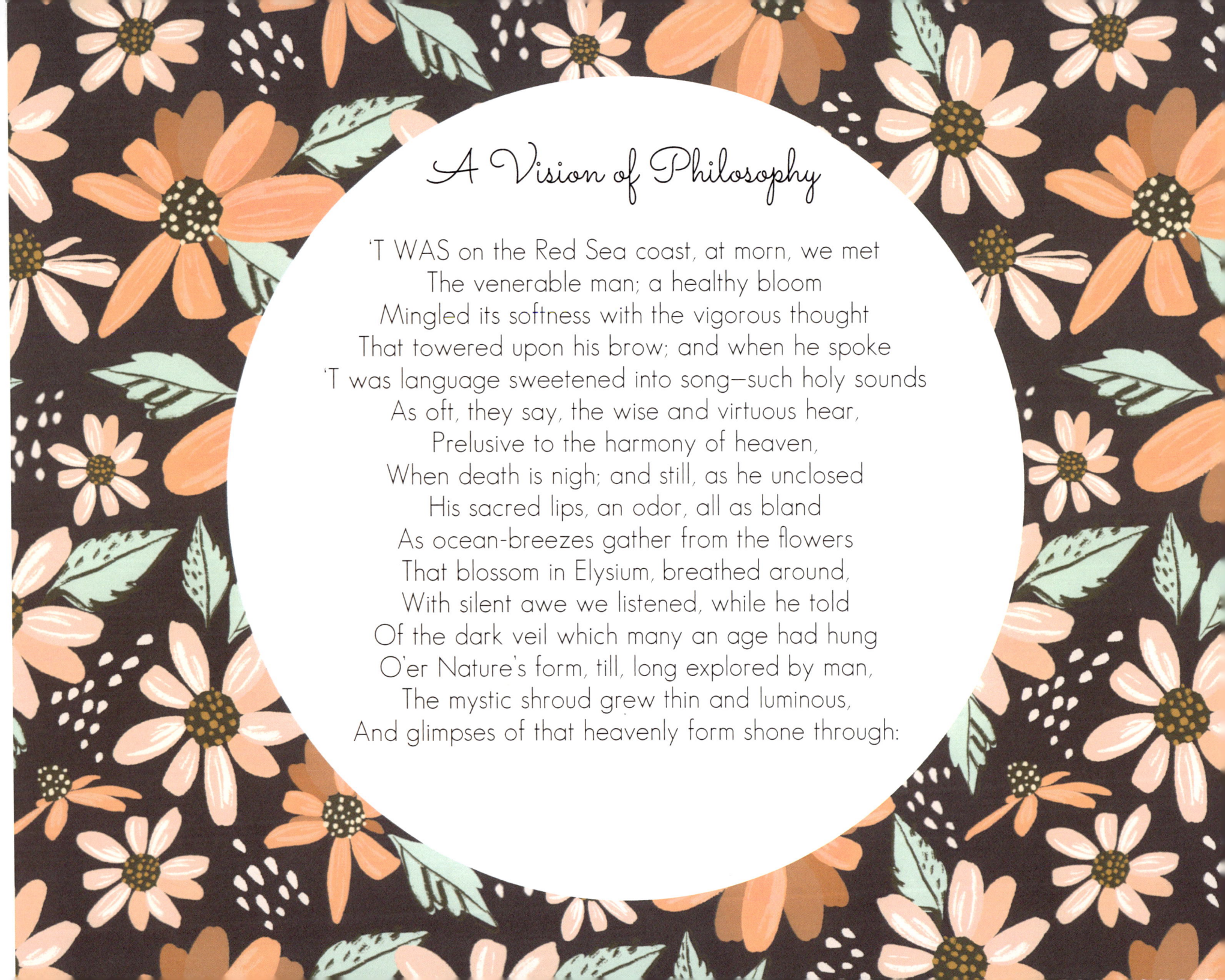

A Vision of Philosophy

'T WAS on the Red Sea coast, at morn, we met
The venerable man; a healthy bloom
Mingled its softness with the vigorous thought
That towered upon his brow; and when he spoke
'T was language sweetened into song—such holy sounds
As oft, they say, the wise and virtuous hear,
Prelusive to the harmony of heaven,
When death is nigh; and still, as he unclosed
His sacred lips, an odor, all as bland
As ocean-breezes gather from the flowers
That blossom in Elysium, breathed around,
With silent awe we listened, while he told
Of the dark veil which many an age had hung
O'er Nature's form, till, long explored by man,
The mystic shroud grew thin and luminous,
And glimpses of that heavenly form shone through:

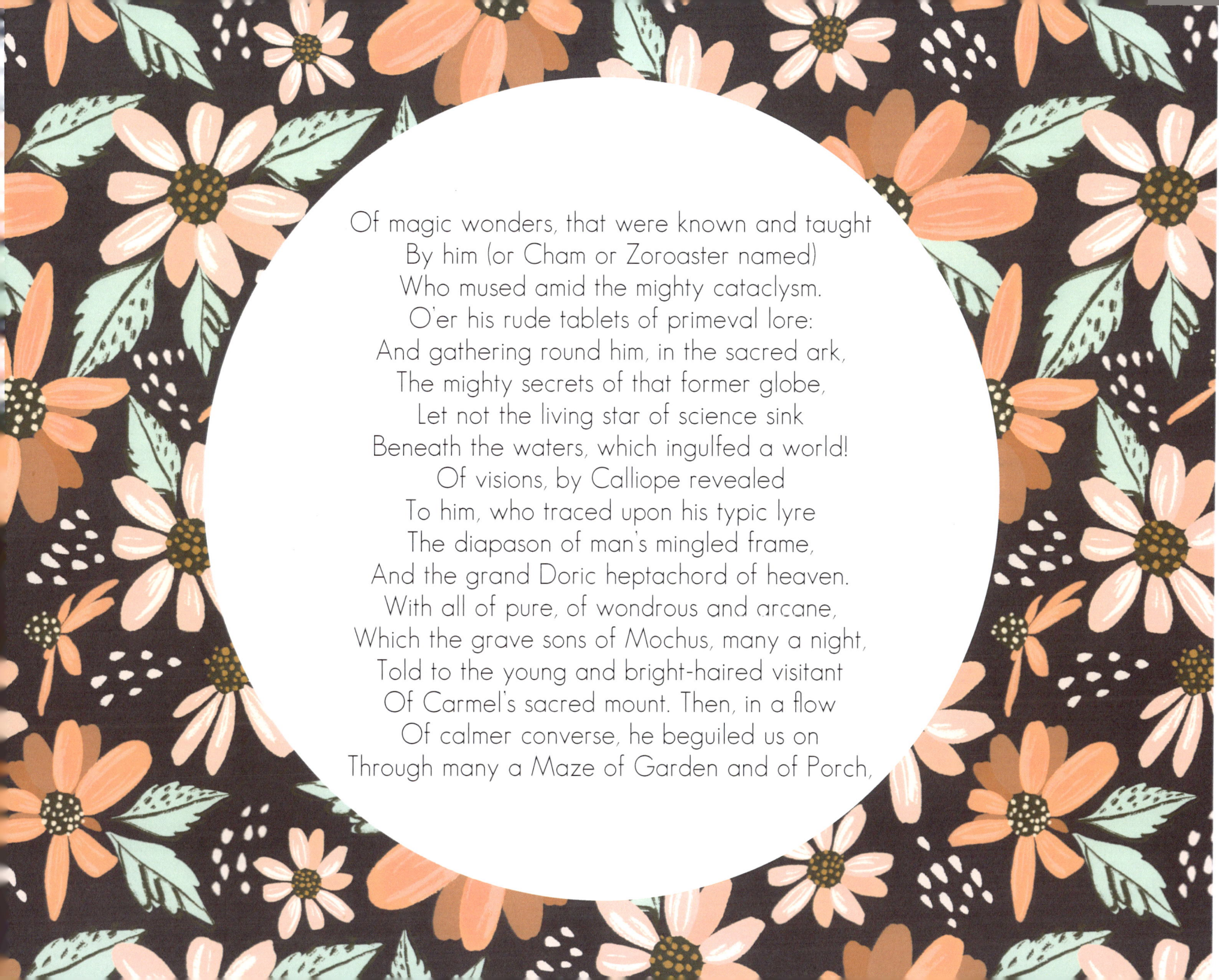

Of magic wonders, that were known and taught
By him (or Cham or Zoroaster named)
Who mused amid the mighty cataclysm.
O'er his rude tablets of primeval lore:
And gathering round him, in the sacred ark,
The mighty secrets of that former globe,
Let not the living star of science sink
Beneath the waters, which ingulfed a world!
Of visions, by Calliope revealed
To him, who traced upon his typic lyre
The diapason of man's mingled frame,
And the grand Doric heptachord of heaven.
With all of pure, of wondrous and arcane,
Which the grave sons of Mochus, many a night,
Told to the young and bright-haired visitant
Of Carmel's sacred mount. Then, in a flow
Of calmer converse, he beguiled us on
Through many a Maze of Garden and of Porch,

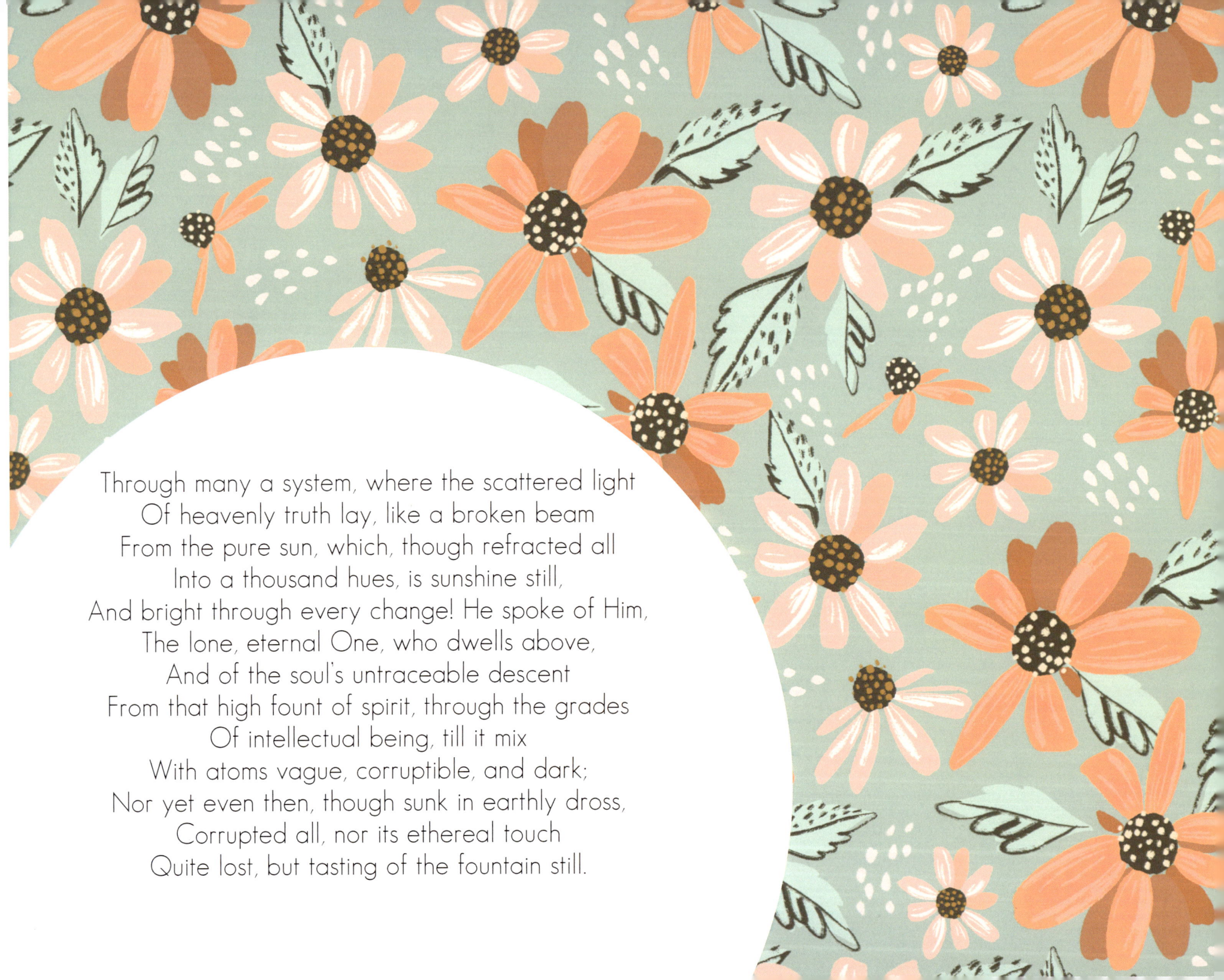

Through many a system, where the scattered light
Of heavenly truth lay, like a broken beam
From the pure sun, which, though refracted all
Into a thousand hues, is sunshine still,
And bright through every change! He spoke of Him,
The lone, eternal One, who dwells above,
And of the soul's untraceable descent
From that high fount of spirit, through the grades
Of intellectual being, till it mix
With atoms vague, corruptible, and dark;
Nor yet even then, though sunk in earthly dross,
Corrupted all, nor its ethereal touch
Quite lost, but tasting of the fountain still.

As some bright river, which has rolled along
Through meads of flowery light and mines of gold,
When poured at length into the dusky deep,
Disdains to take at once its briny taint,
Or balmy freshness, of the scenes it left.
But keeps unchanged awhile the lustrous tinge.
And here the old man ceased, a winged train
Of nymphs and genii bore him from our eyes.
The fair illusion fled! and, as I waked.
'T was clear that my rapt soul had roamed, the while,
To that bright realm of dreams, that spirit-world,
Which mortals know by its long track of light
O'er midnight's sky, and call the Galaxy.

Thomas Moore

A Psalm of Life

Tell me not, in mournful numbers,
Life is but an empty dream!
For the soul is dead that slumbers,
And things are not what they seem.

Life is real! Life is earnest!
And the grave is not its goal;
Dust thou art, to dust returnest,
Was not spoken of the soul.

Not enjoyment, and not sorrow,
Is our destined end or way;
But to act, that each to-morrow
Find us farther than to-day.

Art is long, and Time is fleeting,
And our hearts, though stout and brave,
Still, like muffled drums, are beating
Funeral marches to the grave.

In the world's broad field of battle,
    In the bivouac of Life,
Be not like dumb, driven cattle!
    Be a hero in the strife!

Trust no Future, howe'er pleasant!
    Let the dead Past bury its dead!
Act, act in the living Present!
    Heart within, and God o'erhead!

Lives of great men all remind us
    We can make our lives sublime,
And, departing, leave behind us
    Footprints on the sands of time;

Footprints, that perhaps another,
    Sailing o'er life's solemn main,
A forlorn and shipwrecked brother,
    Seeing, shall take heart again.

Let us, then, be up and doing,
    With a heart for any fate;
Still achieving, still pursuing,
    Learn to labor and to wait.

Henry Wadsworth Longfellow

On Joy and Sorrow

Then a woman said, Speak to us of Joy and Sorrow.
And he answered:
Your joy is your sorrow unmasked.
And the selfsame well from which your laughter rises
was oftentimes filled with your tears.
And how else can it be?
The deeper that sorrow carves into your being, the
more joy you can contain.
Is not the cup that holds your wine the very cup that
was burned in the potter's oven?
And is not the lute that soothes your spirit, the very
wood that was hollowed with knives?
When you are joyous, look deep into your heart
and you shall find it is only that which has given you
sorrow that is giving you joy.

When you are sorrowful look again in your heart,
and you shall see that in truth you are weeping
for that which has been your delight.
Some of you say, "Joy is greater than sorrow,"
and others say, "Nay, sorrow is the greater."
But I say unto you, they are inseparable.
Together they come, and when one sits alone
with you at your board, remember that the other
is asleep upon your bed.
Verily you are suspended like scales between
your sorrow and your joy.
Only when you are empty are you at
standstill and balanced.
When the treasure-keeper lifts you to weigh his
gold and his silver, needs must your joy or your
sorrow rise or fall.

Kahlil Gibran

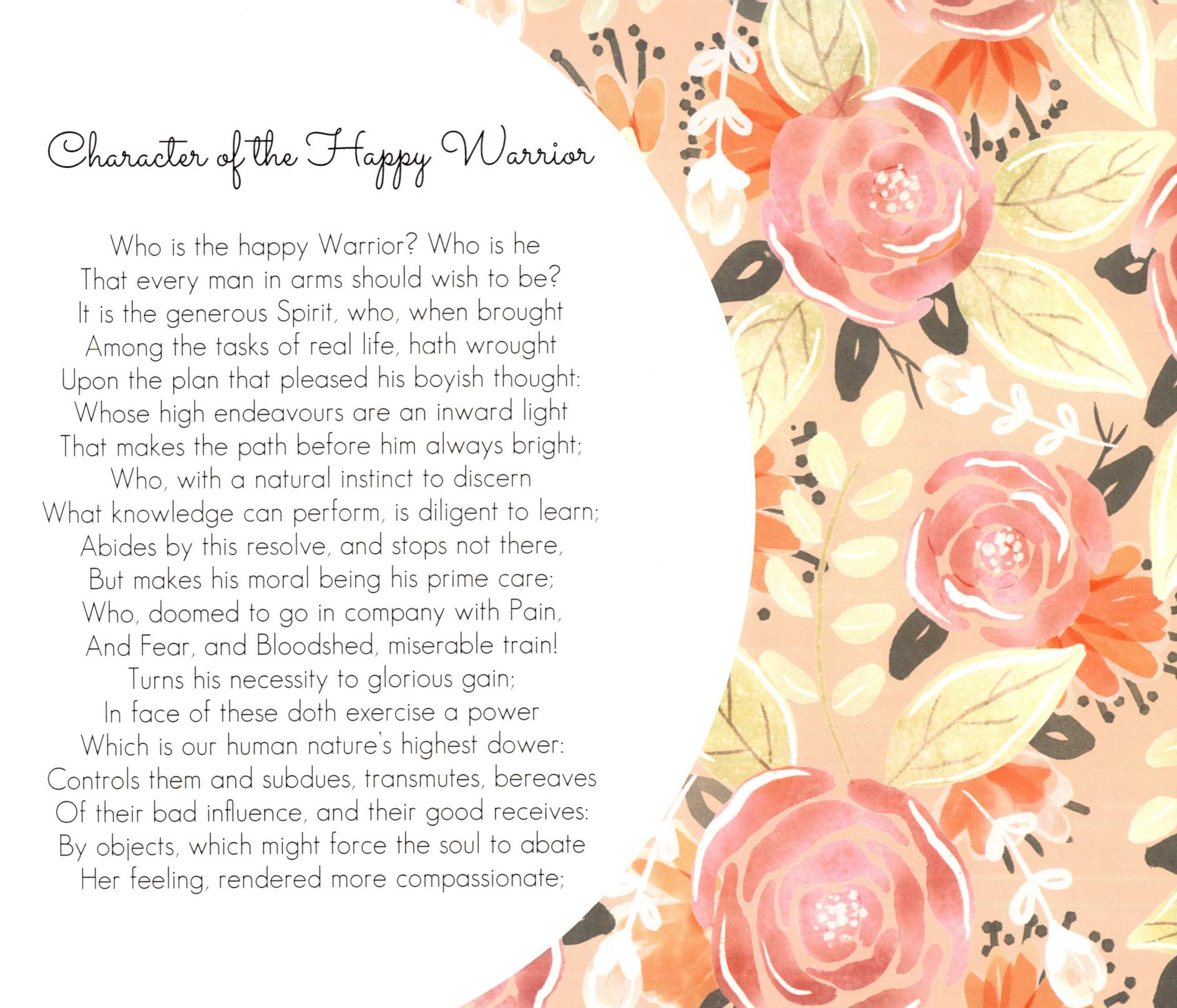

Character of the Happy Warrior

Who is the happy Warrior? Who is he
That every man in arms should wish to be?
It is the generous Spirit, who, when brought
Among the tasks of real life, hath wrought
Upon the plan that pleased his boyish thought:
Whose high endeavours are an inward light
That makes the path before him always bright;
Who, with a natural instinct to discern
What knowledge can perform, is diligent to learn;
Abides by this resolve, and stops not there,
But makes his moral being his prime care;
Who, doomed to go in company with Pain,
And Fear, and Bloodshed, miserable train!
Turns his necessity to glorious gain;
In face of these doth exercise a power
Which is our human nature's highest dower:
Controls them and subdues, transmutes, bereaves
Of their bad influence, and their good receives:
By objects, which might force the soul to abate
Her feeling, rendered more compassionate;

Is placable because occasions rise
So often that demand such sacrifice;
More skilful in self-knowledge, even more pure,
As tempted more; more able to endure,
As more exposed to suffering and distress;
Thence, also, more alive to tenderness.
'Tis he whose law is reason; who depends
Upon that law as on the best of friends;
Whence, in a state where men are tempted still
To evil for a guard against worse ill,
And what in quality or act is best
Doth seldom on a right foundation rest,
He labours good on good to fix, and owes
To virtue every triumph that he knows:
Who, if he rise to station of command,
Rises by open means; and there will stand
On honourable terms, or else retire,
And in himself possess his own desire;

Who comprehends his trust, and to the same
Keeps faithful with a singleness of aim;
And therefore does not stoop, nor lie in wait
For wealth, or honours, or for worldly state;
Whom they must follow; on whose head must fall,
Like showers of manna, if they come at all:
Whose powers shed round him in the common strife,
Or mild concerns of ordinary life,
A constant influence, a peculiar grace;
But who, if he be called upon to face
Some awful moment to which Heaven has joined
Great issues, good or bad for human kind,
Is happy as a Lover; and attired
With sudden brightness, like a Man inspired;
And, through the heat of conflict, keeps the law
In calmness made, and sees what he foresaw;
Or if an unexpected call succeed,
Come when it will, is equal to the need:
He who, though thus endued as with a sense
And faculty for storm and turbulence,
Is yet a Soul whose master-bias leans
To homefelt pleasures and to gentle scenes;
Sweet images! which, wheresoe'er he be,
Are at his heart; and such fidelity

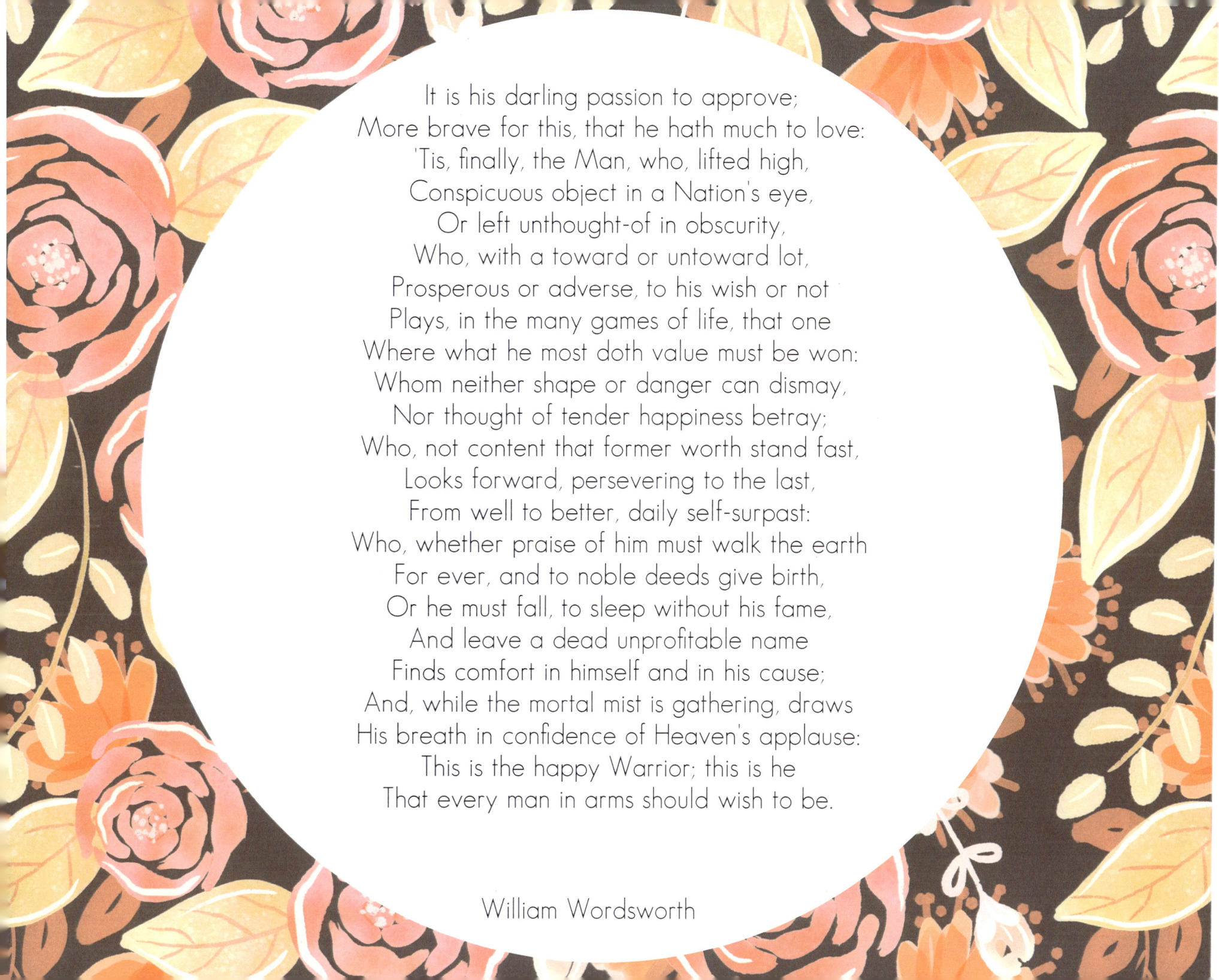

It is his darling passion to approve;
More brave for this, that he hath much to love:
'Tis, finally, the Man, who, lifted high,
Conspicuous object in a Nation's eye,
Or left unthought-of in obscurity,
Who, with a toward or untoward lot,
Prosperous or adverse, to his wish or not
Plays, in the many games of life, that one
Where what he most doth value must be won:
Whom neither shape or danger can dismay,
Nor thought of tender happiness betray;
Who, not content that former worth stand fast,
Looks forward, persevering to the last,
From well to better, daily self-surpast:
Who, whether praise of him must walk the earth
For ever, and to noble deeds give birth,
Or he must fall, to sleep without his fame,
And leave a dead unprofitable name
Finds comfort in himself and in his cause;
And, while the mortal mist is gathering, draws
His breath in confidence of Heaven's applause:
This is the happy Warrior; this is he
That every man in arms should wish to be.

William Wordsworth

To Victory Nike

O Powerful Victory, by men desir'd,
with adverse breasts to dreadful fury fir'd,
Thee I invoke, whose might alone can quell contending rage,
and molestation fell:
'Tis thine in battle to confer the crown,
the victor's prize, the mark of sweet renown;
For thou rul'st all things, Victory divine!
And glorious strife, and joyful shouts are thine.
Come, mighty Goddess, and thy suppliant bless,
with sparkling eye, elated with success;
May deeds illustrious thy protection claim, and find,
led on by thee immortal Fame.

The Hymns of Orpheus
Translated byThomas Taylor

Thinking

If you think you are beaten, you are
If you think you dare not, you don't,
If you like to win, but you think you can't
It is almost certain you won't.

If you think you'll lose, you're lost
For out of the world we find,
Success begins with a fellow's will
It's all in the state of mind.

If you think you are outclassed, you are
You've got to think high to rise,
You've got to be sure of yourself before
You can ever win a prize.

Life's battles don't always go
To the stronger or faster man,
But soon or late the man who wins
Is the man WHO THINKS HE CAN!

Walter D. Wintle

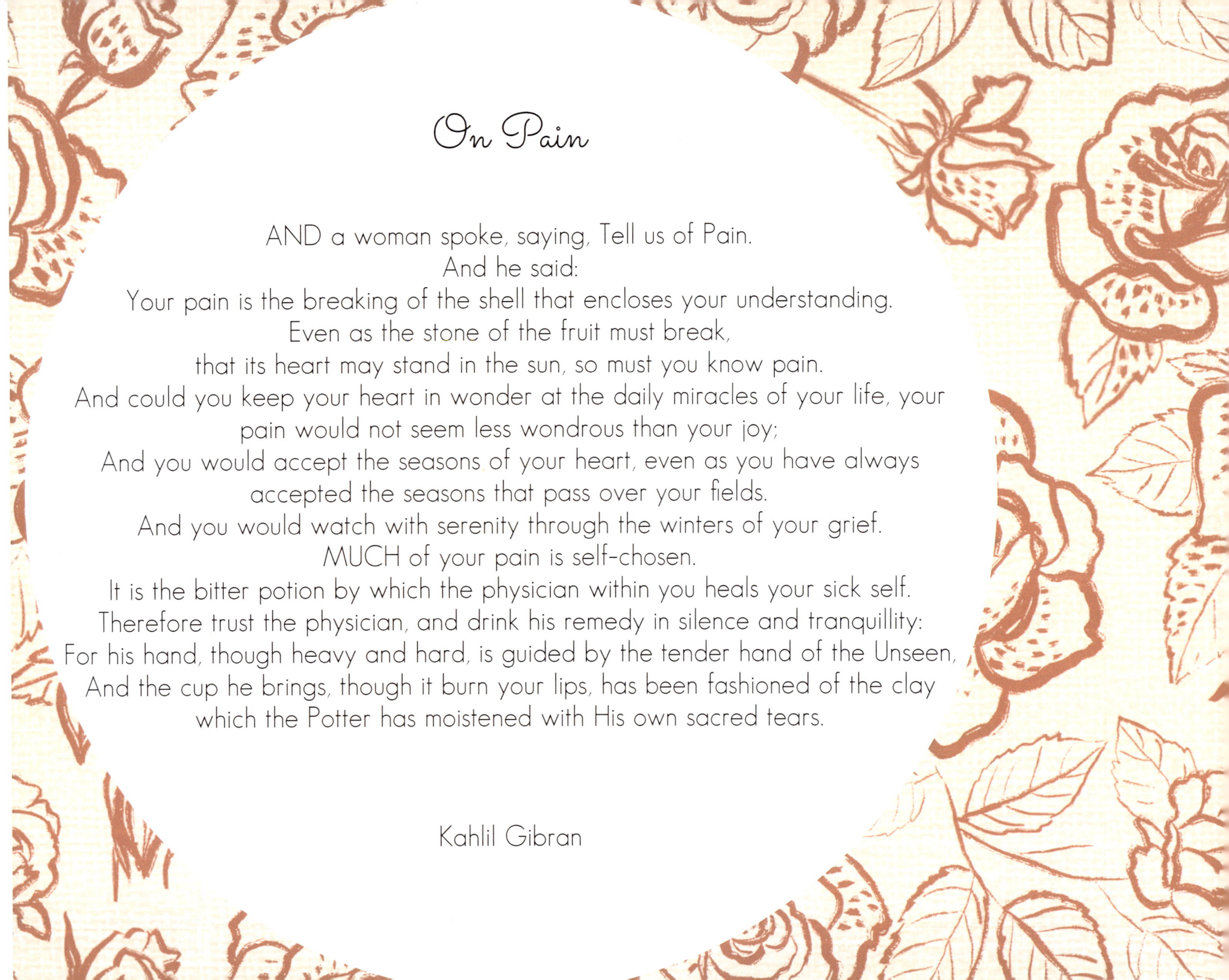

On Pain

AND a woman spoke, saying, Tell us of Pain.
And he said:
Your pain is the breaking of the shell that encloses your understanding.
Even as the stone of the fruit must break,
that its heart may stand in the sun, so must you know pain.
And could you keep your heart in wonder at the daily miracles of your life, your
pain would not seem less wondrous than your joy;
And you would accept the seasons of your heart, even as you have always
accepted the seasons that pass over your fields.
And you would watch with serenity through the winters of your grief.
MUCH of your pain is self-chosen.
It is the bitter potion by which the physician within you heals your sick self.
Therefore trust the physician, and drink his remedy in silence and tranquillity:
For his hand, though heavy and hard, is guided by the tender hand of the Unseen,
And the cup he brings, though it burn your lips, has been fashioned of the clay
which the Potter has moistened with His own sacred tears.

Kahlil Gibran

Hope

Hope is the thing with feathers
That perches in the soul,
And sings the tune without the words,
And never stops at all,

And sweetest in the gale is heard;
And sore must be the storm
That could abash the little bird
That kept so many warm.

I 've heard it in the chillest land,
And on the strangest sea;
Yet, never, in extremity,
It asked a crumb of me.

Emily Elizabeth Dickinson

Self-Knowledge

AND a man said, Speak to us of Self-Knowledge.
And he answered, saying:
Your hearts know in silence the secrets of the days and the nights.
But your ears thirst for the sound of your heart's knowledge.
You would know in words that which you have always known in thought.
You would touch with your fingers the naked body of your dreams.
AND it is well you should.
The hidden well-spring of your soul must needs rise and run murmuring to the sea;
And the treasure of your infinite depths would be revealed to your eyes.
But let there be no scales to weigh your unknown treasure;

And seek not the depths of your knowledge with staff or sounding
line. For self is a sea boundless and measureless.
SAY not, "I have found the truth," but rather, "I have found a truth."
Say not, "I have found the path of the soul."
Say rather, "I have met the soul walking upon my path."
For the soul walks upon all paths.
The soul walks not upon a line, neither does it grow like a reed.
The soul unfolds itself, like a lotus of countless petals.

Kahlil Gibran

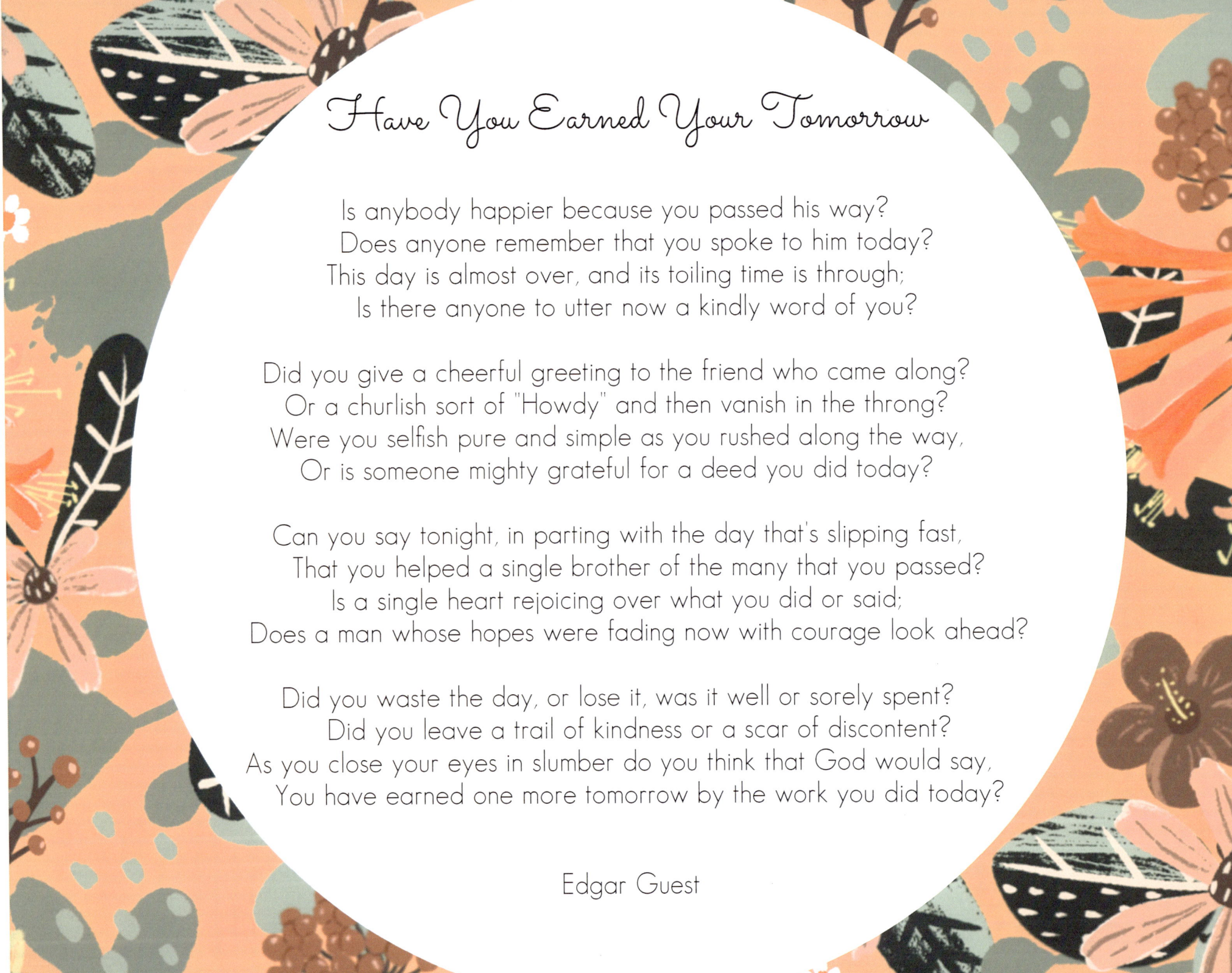

Have You Earned Your Tomorrow

Is anybody happier because you passed his way?
Does anyone remember that you spoke to him today?
This day is almost over, and its toiling time is through;
Is there anyone to utter now a kindly word of you?

Did you give a cheerful greeting to the friend who came along?
Or a churlish sort of "Howdy" and then vanish in the throng?
Were you selfish pure and simple as you rushed along the way,
Or is someone mighty grateful for a deed you did today?

Can you say tonight, in parting with the day that's slipping fast,
That you helped a single brother of the many that you passed?
Is a single heart rejoicing over what you did or said;
Does a man whose hopes were fading now with courage look ahead?

Did you waste the day, or lose it, was it well or sorely spent?
Did you leave a trail of kindness or a scar of discontent?
As you close your eyes in slumber do you think that God would say,
You have earned one more tomorrow by the work you did today?

Edgar Guest

When You Are Old

When you are old and grey and full of sleep,
And nodding by the fire, take down this book,
And slowly read, and dream of the soft look
Your eyes had once, and of their shadows deep;

How many loved your moments of glad grace,
And loved your beauty with love false or true,
But one man loved the pilgrim soul in you,
And loved the sorrows of your changing face;

And bending down beside the glowing bars,
Murmur, a little sadly, how Love fled
And paced upon the mountains overhead
And hid his face amid a crowd of stars.

William Butler Yeats

CPSIA information can be obtained
at www.ICGtesting.com
Printed in the USA
BVRC100954120622
639489BV00016B/69